THREE SCORE TEN

THREE SCORE TEN

Reflections on Aging and the End of Life

M. R. Mercer

RESOURCE *Publications* · Eugene, Oregon

THREE SCORE AND TEN
Reflections on Aging and the End of Life

Resource Publications
An Imprint of Wipf and Stock Publishers
199 W. 8th Ave., Suite 3
Eugene, OR 97401

www.wipfandstock.com

PAPERBACK ISBN: 978-1-5326-5680-4
HARDCOVER ISBN: 978-1-5326-5681-1
EBOOK ISBN: 978-1-5326-5682-8

Manufactured in the U.S.A.   09/12/18

TABLE OF CONTENTS

INTRODUCTION

OUR WESTERN CULTURE SEEMS pretty deeply mired in a climate of denial. Whether it is our failure to recognize that we enjoy a land of plenty in a world where most people suffer lives of least, or whether we revel in the preciousness of our individuality at the expense of any appreciation of the other, we miss the meaning of our humanity time and time again. Maybe the most egregious shortcoming we share is the denial of our mortality. We dedicate billions of dollars every year in search of youthful appearance and an avoidance of aging. It is unfortunately to our peril as human beings that we fail to engage the reality of our mortality, to recognize that we are creatures who have limits. One can come to one's later years never having faced this looming reality, and never having benefitted from accepting this crucial human factor.

The reflections that follow are a record of some of my own thoughts and struggles as I've engaged the inevitability of my mortality. To that extent they are quite personal at times, but I hope they will echo the thoughts of many readers at "my time of life!" It's my hope that by sharing these thoughts I will encourage more people to be serious about the reality of his or her life. I believe such reflection carries the possibility of helping us to face up to the limits of life and to stop the "immortality momentum" that so many allow to fool them into denial. My hope, then, is that it will no longer allow us to postpone healthy understandings about life's purpose and how faith functions helpfully in our lives.

INTRODUCTION

These pieces are in large part quite humble attempts to be honest about my own struggles in this topic and to share openly where I find myself at this point in my life. I can say that I began this exercise trying to speak simply as a human being apart from my personal faith convictions. I still believe that all beings need to do this reflective work. I must confess at the conclusion of this writing that I could not personally manage these reflections apart from the context of my own faith convictions. I leave it to the reader to engage his or her work in this matter. Perhaps faith will need "to become part of the inner dialogue" for them as well.

A.

Ambition

IT MIGHT SEEM A little odd to begin a series of reflections on aging with "ambition." After all, at this point in my life I'm not at all sure what future, personal goals could possibly be named. That's the struggle. As I reflect on my life, I realize that I've been more ambitious than I knew at the time. The desire to make a difference in the human circumstance has always driven me to perform, in addition to a family-formed ethic that was always more interested in what remained undone than in what had been accomplished already. In its most potent and rawest form, I suppose that ambition is actually an idolatry of the self in which your own goals and agenda place you at the centre of everything. As I age, I find myself more and more at the periphery of the "action," and it is becoming harder and harder to see myself as crucial to any endeavor. The reality, of course, is that none of us is ever at the centre of things; that place is taken by the creator of all, and always has been. If aging and "golden years" have any deep benefit, and there are many days when I struggle to know that they do, it's that they have the potential of helping us to see God as the centre of life. If that's true, then that relationship of faith is even more important than I have practiced it throughout my life. It should change the agenda and re-shape the focus of ambition at the very least.

Three Score Ten

Strive first for the kingdom of God and His righteousness
and all these things wills be given to you as well.
[Matt.6.33 NRSV]

B.

Baptism

IN THE RITE OF initiation, Christians–and in a brave extension of the promise, their infants–are symbolically and spiritually incorporated into Christ. They die with Christ in the waters of Baptism and are then raised to new life, resurrected as it were to become inheritors of the Kingdom of God. All we know of life, death and new life is encapsulated in baptism. In a real sense it tells the whole story for a Christian; it's a story we learn over and over in each baptism.

It's a story to recall as one considers the last years of our earthly lives as well, because it's a story containing an immense promise of continuance, and eternal permanence with God. Our story continues after our earthly passing, just as we prefigure our resurrection as we come out of the waters of baptism renewed and received into the Reign of God–a reign which is inaugurated through our participation in Christ, but that continues through the end of this age into eternity.

> We were therefore buried with him through baptism into
> death in order that, just as Christ was raised from the dead
> through the glory of the Father, we too may live a new life.
> [Romans 6.4 NIV]

Belonging

A FUNDAMENTAL DRIVE IN the human creature is the need to belong. It is important to each of us to be part of something larger than us, to be integral to a meaning that extends far beyond us. It has been said that this desire to belong can be broken down into some component parts. Those components point to our desire to be important as individuals, to have meaning and significance; we also want to feel some connection to the eternal; and, of course, we desire to be embedded in human community. In other words we wish to belong to created order and to have our place in it; we wish to be connected to our God; and, we desperately need to be connected to each other. If any of these parameters are disordered, we do not feel we belong properly.

> *So then you are no longer strangers and aliens, but you are*
> *citizens with the saints and also members of the household*
> *of God. [Eph. 2.1; NRSV]*

C.

Cardinal

As the Spring hovers in the wings of creation's stage, the male cardinal in my yard is getting ready. Everyday, it seems, the bird is more and more brilliantly red and somehow seems to radiate expectancy. His partner continues to be present and attentive, but is not evolving colorfully beyond the steady olive that she seems to display all year. It's as if the male has a dimmer switch that he releases a little each day as the breeding season approaches, a season when attractiveness and territory matter.

It all reminds me of a bride preparing for her wedding! As the day nears, more and more of the planning and preparation is completed so that the big day will dawn with everything ready for the beginning of a new life and partnership.

I must confess that, as I think and prepare for the big day in which my new life will begin, I feel pretty dowdy and fatigued by the vagaries of this present life in which the body is more tired and more seems wrong with it - sore hips, aching hands and so on. Maybe what I need is a conversation with the cardinal about seeing the future more creatively, and getting dressed up for it!

> ... for a bird of the air will carry your voice
> Or some winged creature tell the matter. [Eccl. 10.4 ESV]

Change

ONE OF THE REALITIES that has marked my life is "change," and on almost every front! In times of transition, and I've had several of those, change can often feel very sharp and difficult, and not something creative or life-giving. As I've experienced transition from one segment of life to another, from one calling to another, from one community to another, the interim time can feel disorienting, dysfunctional and downright uncomfortable.

THIS HAS ALSO BEEN true in my inner life as I've responded to different situations and circumstances around me. As a Christian, if the New Testament is to be my guide, I am urged to be constantly growing and developing as I aspire to be Christ-like. This means that change is to be my constant companion as I follow along my path of faith. My temptation, however, is often to try to settle into comfortable valleys of stasis in which nothing changes, and where I can manage it so that it stays that way. I want to be in control. This is not God's intention for me; I know inside there's much more for me to become. There's much more of God's fullness and love to experience, and there's much more ministry in which I'm to engage. In this sense, Christians don't ever retire!

How then am I to cope when change is in the air, especially as I engage the reality of aging and end of life issues? Well, I think it's all about my focus. Where do I look, or rather to whom do I look, when I feel the pressures of change and transition? Of course, the answer is to Jesus. Sometimes I feel that I'm saying the obvious when I announce something like that. The truth, though, is that I so often let other things become my focus and I can easily become misguided and more disoriented by looking in the wrong direction. I play golf from time to time and have learned that I must always keep my eye on the ball if I'm going to hit it well; but I usually get distracted and lift my head most of the time and that's why I'm only a duffer on the golf course.

As a Christian I can be a duffer in my faith life, too, by failing to keep my eyes on the Lord. As I grow and change, I must keep my eyes on the One whose sacrifice made my faith possible. I can embrace "change," even at the end of my life, if I keep my eyes on the "ball!"

> . . . let us run with perseverance the race marked out for us. [Heb. 12. 1 NIV]

Chickadees, Juncos and Nuthatches

As my schedule has eased off in recent weeks, I've found myself taking more time over my morning coffee and observing the tiny birds that are frequenting the several feeders my wife manages at this time of year. The chickadees and nuthatches fly in to roost on the feeders while the juncos tend to feed on the ground where the overflow is deposited by the more frenetic roosters.

They seem to arrive in groups about the same time each morning, perhaps stopping at our place on a well-planned route that leads to other feeders, manned by various neighbours. Nevertheless, they come to us with a kind of abandonment, clearly not feeling that we pose any threat to them. Even though they can see me through the glass, they continue their grazing with no concern other than their need for food.

As I personally agonise over meaning and the reality of my limits, the birds simply take our food thankful for our gift of supply for them. They're not engaged in any esoteric struggle for purpose; they're simply following their natural agenda of being birds and meeting their survival needs and the demand of their breed to put in place the conditions for the success of their next generation.

Perhaps I should think less and just get on with living my life until the time comes for not living any longer. What conditions, for example, can I establish for my next generations? Rather than focusing too much on my issues, I need to look well outside myself more often. "Other" needs to trump "self" more consistently; after all, is that not what living abundantly means?

Even the sparrow finds a home, and the swallow a nest for herself. [Ps. 84.3 NEV]

Claustrophobia

ONE OF THE REALITIES in life, when the time for full-time work has passed, is that one can experience a form of claustrophobia. Your world can seem to shrink when there is less demand to get out and engage it in something like a regular work environment. In the relative safety of your home, you can almost unknowingly retreat from your culture. As your own world gets smaller, you can actually become less able to manage the real world beyond. And the risk of seeking escape from reality looms larger. It can simulate a premature dying and does become habit-forming. The matters of one's own day are smaller than reality and can become more risky if you pursue escape in any number of harmful ways.

The antidote to escape is to choose engagement, to tussle with reality and to find things that channel you into life-giving and purposeful activity. I don't believe that we are meant to live out our later years passively awaiting the end of it all, wrapped up in our own little world.

> . . .forgetting what lies behind and straining forward to
> what lies ahead, I press on toward the goal for the prize of
> the heavenly call of God in Christ Jesus.
> [Phil. 3.13, 14 NRSV]

Confession

FROM TIME TO TIME throughout my pastoral ministry parishioners have asked me to attend acquaintances that were dying and for whatever reason, apparently beyond the pale of the church. They nevertheless needed to talk about what they were experiencing and what lay ahead for them. I visited one woman in her home and she seemed quite cogent and willing to talk with me. The chat seemed to revolve around the events of her life and I engaged them as fully as I was able. The visit took its course and, after an hour and a half or so, I left with an agreement that I would come back the following week to talk further. I did that and the conversation had a similar trajectory, social and reasonably engaged. By my third visit, I confess I was more frustrated by these encounters than perhaps I should have been. After all, this relationship was extra to my regular work responsibilities.

Not long after I arrived, I put it to her that she had asked to see me, but had yet to approach the matter of her dying, the issue she had wanted to discuss. At that point she broke down and finally shared her concern. She felt she had not always done good things in her life, and she was afraid of what God might do with that. She had needed an act of confession before she could let go of the life she had. I assured her that God forgives the penitent and we had a rich time of sharing before I left. She died two days later!

That experience reminds me that confession is a good thing. Clearly this woman was gifted with a time of preparation for her dying and was able to speak of her life regrets in an ultimately redemptive manner. How important it is for each of us to keep our "slate" clean, so to speak. The Twelve-step programs have certainly realized this importance in their process of evaluating one's actions over time, and seeking reconciliation when it is appropriate. I suppose confession really is good for the soul.

> Then I let it all out; I said, "I'll make a clean breast of my failures to God." Suddenly the pressure was gone—my guilt dissolved, my sin disappeared. [Ps. 32.5; The Message]

Courage

THE ACTRESS BETTE DAVIS once declared that, "Growing old is not for sissies!"[1] What she was saying was that it takes courage to engage the process of aging proactively because there are many challenging things about it. Like it or not the struggle to accept our mortality is not an easy or simple thing; it takes a struggle for each of us to end well. That struggle requires us to be brave.

For many of us who are aging, the reality is that we do it with somewhat diminished physical resources; there are compromises to make if we are to thrive. Our bodies "creak" more and we possibly face chronic illness as well.

For most of our adult lives we can be relatively clear about our purpose, whether it be in developing our careers, raising families, acquiring wealth and security, and so on. In later years, we need to re-purpose ourselves for a different kind of life and goal, something we have no experience in and for which no-one seems to offer counsel or support. Certainly, we don't openly talk about or discuss it honestly; it's a relatively private fight and requires us to be resourceful and strong.

We undertake some significant movements in our latter years. For spiritual people, we move from achieving, goals and acquisitions, to trying to rest in God; it is more about "being" than "doing"–I suppose it was always meant to be like that. Instead of seeking and receiving support and wisdom from elders, we find that we are more often the givers of advice and counsel. Our focus shifts from our own journey to that of others, children and grandchildren perhaps, or simply those who seek us out as mentors. It takes courage to change from being self-directed to being at the service of others. Not only do we have personal agenda, and yes struggle, but we are to learn how to be strong for others!

Like long-distance runners, we need to run our race to completion and even to find a finishing "kick!"

Be strong and courageous. Fear not; do not be dismayed.
[I Chron. 22.1;3 ESV]

D.

Deserve . . . Receive

I WAS RECENTLY IN a restaurant having lunch and found, by way of decoration I suppose, five words written large in sequence across the wall: deserve, desire, ask, believe, and receive. I was particularly struck by the order they were in and realized that they were actually descriptive of our current society's confusion. Time and time again, in various advertisements, we are bombarded with the idea that we deserve something. "You deserve a break today"[2] is perhaps the highest profile example, but there are countless other versions as well. As the words on the wall suggest, "deserving" culminates in "receiving" and the cycle of self-gratification rolls on. What we decide we want, we receive; the intermediate steps of desiring, asking, and believing are merely part of the process and have no effect apparent on the outcome.

When my daughter first got access to the family car at sixteen, we began a bit of a dance about when she could use it. She would certainly ask permission, but if for some reason I had to decline, she was upset and indignantly asked why not. She recognized my authority on matters concerning the family vehicle enough to ask, but her compliance disappeared when my answer went against her wishes. In her own mind, I wonder if she didn't feel as if she deserved to use the car; asking permission was just a slippery little part of the process before she received the keys.

The logic of the words on the restaurant wall fails because they have a faulty starting point, one that is steeped in the imagination that the individual is the centre of the universe and everything in it is there to serve that individual. Contrary to this cultural reality, the Christian acknowledges the Creator to be at the centre of things and that none of us deserves anything if not for the goodness and mercy of the God who welcomes us when we accept the right order God has made available. It's God's grace alone that makes us "deserving."

One can imagine that this contemporary "deserve . . . receive" thinking can really throw us off course when we think about our death. I don't suppose there's any moment like our death to highlight the reality that we are not all this creation is about! Even a significant illness can tell us that. If we begin to think we "deserve" to live forever, that is if we even think of death at all, we will find it very hard to face our earthly end in a healthy way. The restaurant's words on the wall, appealing as they might be to contemporary observers, are unable to accommodate the full reality of humanity and serve only to satisfy our consumer mentality. Perhaps it's better to appropriate the right order that includes our limits and the ways in which our Maker has provided for that inevitability.

> *From Christ's fullness we have all received, grace upon grace. [John 1.16; NRSV]*

Diary

It's NOT LONG AGO that my life and its rhythm were dictated by the entries in my diary. Those pages were like the score of a symphony that seemed to have a life of its own sometimes, a life onto which I hung desperately as a player of some bit part. Every entry in my diary demanded a piece of me and consumed the minutes and hours of my days. It defined me so to speak!

At this point in my life, my diary is quite different; it documents pending medical appointments and the increasingly occasional coffee or lunch with someone from the past with which I have some passing currency.

I think there's grief in the empty pages of my diary. I'm tempted to see there my irrelevancy, in the cut and thrust of a valued life in our world, as a loss or deficit in my meaning. Wondering if I don't matter anymore is a question that shadows me in my more thoughtful moments. Are the empty pages simply prophetic of my leaving this life, of my "obituariness?"

This also raises the question of whether I'm afraid to die. Henri Nouwen is helpful when he speaks of being afraid to die. He admits that he's afraid whenever he lets himself be seduced by the noisy voices of his world–read here the pages of his diary?–that tell him his "little life" is all he has and to do it with all urgency.[3] The empty pages of my diary suggest that the noisy voices may have actually already given up on my little life.

The truth is that my diary, full or empty, says nothing about my worth or value in the great scheme of things. Nouwen says that ". . . our few years on this earth are part of a much larger event that

stretches out far beyond the boundaries of our birth and death."[4]
My diary is not designed to document that!!

> *This is the day that the Lord has made; let us rejoice and be glad in it. [Ps.118.24; NRSV]*

Dock Diving

THE DOCK AT THE cottage is raised substantially above the water level late in the summer. Lake entry for swimming requires a leap or a dive, if you're up to that. For years, that was my favourite way to swim in the lake, starting with a majestic dive, as I perceived it at least. It was always a moment when I assumed my young daughters and their cousins watched in wonder at my height defying performance.

Now, I'm a little stiffer and feel it unnecessary to assault the sinuses with such a leap from on high. For me, it's a slower descent on the ladder from the dock. On it, I slip innocuously into the water pausing to test the temperature and avoiding the shock of too fast an entry!

On a recent weekend, I realized that the high-flying lake entry had become the purview of my son-in-law! Everything I used to do in this free unabashed dive into the lake he now does–and with that came an instance of reality for me that I may not have thought about before. Life is moving forward and is in the process of moving on from me to another generation. At first realization, I found this quite anxiety-producing as I thought about the impact of what I was observing. As I reflected on it, however, I came to feel more at peace. The appropriate revolving of the generations is well underway; how can I not feel good about that? My best hope is that my son-in-law will someday stand on the dock and watch his adult son diving into the lake from a great height! It is to that cycle of life that we are all committed.

As for mortals, their days are like grass; they flourish like a flower of the field; for the wind passes over it, and it is gone, and its place knows it no more.

But the steadfast love of the Lord is from everlasting to everlasting on those who fear him, and his righteousness to children's children, to those who keep his covenant and remember to do his commandments.[Ps.103.15-18; NRSV]

Doubt

SINCE THE TIME OF the disciple Thomas, "doubt" has been given a bad rap. It seems clear that Thomas' concern for unquestioned data around his teacher's wounds, and his return from death, is perfectly fine and acceptable to the Risen Jesus. Many argue as do I, that faith and doubt are deeply connected, of the same family in a sense. Neither makes sense without the other. They each individually represent the absence and the presence of a conviction about the truth of something. Without each other they are without context; like it or not, they belong together.

Do not doubt, but believe. [John 20.27 NRSV]

Dreamer

DREAMER WAS A GOLDEN Retriever that shared our lives and hearts for a decade or so. We received him from a friend's sister in northern British Columbia when he was three years old. He had been named "Dreamer" because he seemed to day dream his way through life. It was not his life choice, however, and when he was diagnosed with a thyroid condition, it meant that his breeding potential had gone. So our good friend Judy, a dedicated "dog-lady," travelled out west to meet her sister and bring Dreamer back to our family.

Dreamer had been an obedience champion in his earlier years and integrated really well with life in our home. Not that there weren't adjustments to make, certainly for us if not for the dog. Dreamer was a "suck" and would cozy up to anyone who would show him kindness and affection: a guard dog he was not! But as a rectory dog, he was wonderful with children who came to the house and visitors in general.

I became very attached to the dog and Dreamer became an important part of our family. I have very warm memories of him curled up in my lap on a lounge chair on the decks of two different houses over time. In fact, Dreamer seemed to expect the benefits of being a human in the family; I wonder if I became more dog-like at the same time.

In those years, we used to take holidays in a small camper van, usually on the east coast and Dreamer came too. Once he understood that he could not sit on the driver's lap–I doubt he ever truly accepted that–the trips became pleasurable. He loved the ocean and insisted on drinking it even though it usually made him vomit! On hot summer days, he celebrated the cooling effect of the ocean and would just stand in the water reveling in the feeling of not being panting hot.

On our last trip east with Dreamer, when my wife and I were alone and the girls were in university with their summers full and engaged, it became clear to us that he wasn't well. He lost his appetite and nothing we could do enticed him to eat. This is the same dog that once ate all the girls' Halloween candy–he was passing silver wrappers for days afterwards–and steaks off the counter when we weren't alert. So when he lost his appetite, we knew something was not right.

The vet said he had cancer, and we were left with the realization that life was not good anymore for Dreamer. The day we put him down was not a good day for me or my wife. I took him to the vet and while he once more curled up in my lap on the floor she injected him with a final dose. He died gently in my arms.

As I recall that moment, even years later, I still feel sadness and grief. At the same time, I want to honour the way in which Dreamer stoically dealt with his illness, and the way he died. I don't really know, but I'm pretty sure he knew what that final trip to the vet was about. He accepted the final intimacy of that contact with me and died in the assurance of being loved. I wonder if we all should die that way, no matter of the circumstantial suffering we may experience. To know we're loved by our families, and certainly by our Creator who awaits us. I wonder if I'll die like Dreamer.

Precious in the sight of the Lord is the death of his faithful ones.[Ps. 116.15; NRSV]

Dying to live

I ARRIVED IN THE parish in Lent and my family moved into the rectory after school was out in June. During those months I commuted while I tried to get to know the community. The first day back from my July holiday, a parishioner and her friend arrived in my office. Her husband had had some primary cancer dealt with before I'd arrived; now it had returned as liver cancer and he had a limited time to be cared for palliatively. His wife, who was a nurse, wanted to care for him at home; thus began the most meaningful human journey I think I have taken. About sixty members of the parish shared in some form of support for the family, whether it was taking him to the coffee shop (latterly bringing him coffee), providing meals, giving respite to his wife or helping out with two teenagers who probably were pretty overwhelmed by what was happening at home.

In my desire to make this dying a healthy one in which the family was engaged and supported, I met weekly with the gathered family to help them sort out their feelings and concerns, their fears and their anxieties. In my first pastoral charge as the chief pastor, I was flying by the knees of the pants on which I prayed a lot. No seminary training could have prepared me for my role in this dying. This experience cast a shadow over the whole church and every program. Church school teachers met in planning meetings and asked me how they could teach Gospel stories about healing while their friend was dying. Others wanted to know how, or if, healing worked in this case. I had no answer other than my conviction that our Christian task was to seek good news in the midst of bad.

In addition to the family meetings, I also spent lots of time with the man himself; it was hard work and I made mistakes. One bears repeating. It happened in the living room during the day. He was lying on one arm engaging me in conversation and, as usual, I was committed to talking proactively about the matter at hand. In the middle of some pastoral missile, he leaned up further and looked me in the eye with some fervour and said, "Merv, will you stop killing me off before I'm f----ing gone!!"

I was humbled by his challenge, because I wanted to live in his death, and he needed to die in his life: I had the wrong perspective altogether. Even when we die, let alone age through the Golden years, we want and need to live each day as fully as possible. That's what abundant life is, I suppose.

> *I came that they may have life, and have it to the fullest.*
> *[John 10.10; NIV]*

E.

Enemy

ANY CHRISTIAN WHO IS unaware of the reality of evil and the activity of an enemy is naïve and runs the risk of foundering. Now, I don't want to be dramatic or appear Medieval about this; I'm not someone to imagine evil spirits around every corner. It's obvious to me, though, that the redemptive enterprise in which we participate with Christ is of such a scale that it causes the opposite side of the cosmic struggle to be concerned about us, about you, about me.

I CAN SEE NO half measure in how we must go about our faith enterprise. Either we believe wholeheartedly in our God, or we may as well go golfing. And if we are true to our faith, then we must accept that Christ engaged powers and principalities that wanted to keep creation broken. The groaning for the new creation that Paul describes in Romans 8.22 is something we too must hear.

If we're engaged in such a struggle, it should not be surprising that the end of life is going to involves skirmishes with our enemy. Those may take the shape of fear, of doubt, or anything that can turn our face from the "forever future" that God has planned for us. We might even expect our last years to be more intense than any others in terms of the warfare I've described; after all, our dying is in a sense the final battle in which we choose faith, or not. It is the enemy's last chance to turn us from our rightful destiny with God.

I expect that it's important to ask for protection from this kind of assault and not to minimize its reality. It's not something I will yell from the rooftops - that's not my style - but in my heart, it will be close practice.

The last enemy to be destroyed is death.
[1 Cor.15.26; NRSV]

F.

Family

I AM FROM A small, nuclear and immigrant family; I had no siblings and any extended family were thousands of miles remote. I was also born into a clergy home with an old-fashioned understanding of leadership that frowned on too much fraternization with the people in the church in which you were currently offering leadership. I doubt this made me the introvert I am, but it did mean a number of other things. It made me dependant on my imagination for my amusement, whether playing backyard games on my own, or delving into the world of books and reading. Some might see my childhood as lonely because of this; however, it did have its good sides.

When I married, it was into what I considered a very large family. There were four siblings in my wife's immediate family and many uncles and aunts and cousins and so on. The Annual Family picnic, which continues to this day at the original, Confederation family farm, is now well over one hundred and twenty people, and further complicated by failed marriages, second partners and a steady stream of children from generation to generation! I find it overwhelming!

My wife and I have two children who have produced three children of their own now, and I find my thinking is undergoing a revision. I'm still an introvert and have my limits in entertaining the family, but I think I'm finally appreciating the richness of our whole family sitting at the dining table, each one connected to the other in a deep and profound way. Finally, I'm embedded in an extended family. Even as a father I somehow did not appreciate what I was living through in the way I now celebrate my "papa-ness."

As an aging grandparent, I now reflect on how much of the grandchildren's lives I will be around to enjoy. Mortality even seems to breathe on my happy discovery of "family!"

The Lord exists forever; your word is firmly fixed in heaven. Your faithfulness endures to all generations.
[Ps.119. 89.90; NRSV]

Fear

IT DOESN'T SEEM TO matter how firm your faith is, the moment of death carries with it a tangible fear, at least if you are aware of what is happening. To the extent that I've imagined this moment I must confess that I worry about whatever that "crossing over" is going to be like; frankly, it frightens me. Will I die well? Will my faith hold up to that event?

In my pastoral ministry I've encountered many individuals in their time of passing, but none of them affected me like Lu. Lu had been a parish secretary two ministers before I had arrived, and although she had basically retired, she did understand my job and the pressures that went with it. Lu's home was the place I went when I needed support and understanding; there was always a cup of tea with a large dose of listening and fellowship.

One of the early deficits I identified in my bag of pastoral gifts was a lack of personal experience with death. Apart from tragically losing my dog when I was fourteen, I'd never lost "someone" close; actually, that loss bore eerily similar qualities to losses I have experienced subsequently. As I dealt with deaths in the community, I decided to ask Lu for help. She had been widowed suddenly as a young woman with a son, and had lived out her days on her own. I went to see her with my problem and asked her to tell me about death and the experience she had when her husband had died.

She recounted the utter devastation she had felt at his loss, the helplessness and depression. This did not describe the Lu I knew and so I asked her what had helped her. Her answer was to describe an experience that to this day I cannot explain or find theological categories for. She said that one night not long after her husband's death he appeared at the end of her bed and told her to come with him. She went with him to a car parked in the driveway; her mother was sitting in the back seat. And they drove. Eventually they came to a hilltop overlooking what Lu described as an unspeakably beautiful valley; she and her husband got out. He told her that this was where they were and that she must not worry for them; they were just fine in this beautiful place. Then, he said he needed to take her back home; she, of course, refused to leave, but he convinced her there was no choice and that this was not her time.

As she described it for me, she woke the next morning essentially healed from her grief and was not disabled by it ever again. Lu gave me permission to tell this story whenever it may be helpful, but I still don't understand it!

A few years later, a clearly aging Lu took me aside briefly at church on Sunday and asked if I'd drop by during the week. Of course, I did just that. When I asked her what was wrong, she said to me, "I'm afraid of dying!" Not knowing how to help with that, I asked her to tell me again the story of her encounter with her dead husband. And as she retold that story, I saw her relief growing and her "healing" taking hold. I still could not find theological validation for her story; but I could not deny its effect.

Lu fought recurring cancer a number of times and my visits to her seemed to be more likely in the hospital than anywhere else. Some years later, she was once more in hospital but in a more extreme condition. I remember my last visit with her there. She was a rabid fan of the city's baseball team, so our personal liturgy always involved an initial catch-up on the team's current performance. Knowing her death was close, I eventually asked her if she was afraid. We both knew what I asked, and her answer was a brisk "a little." And then she immediately asked me to rub her neck! That was our last conversation; she died two hours later!

As I reflect on death today, my death I suppose, I wonder what Lu's experience might mean for me. I think it's true that death is a mystery and that, like anything unclear, it leaves us unsure of the reality of the experience. We don't know what that moment will hold for us; but Christians at least need to be as clear as we're able to be about the destination we have before us. Fear is alright as we face death; but it's a fear that is coated in hope and confidence. That is what Lu taught me, even if my theological categories fail me when I try to explain these experiences.

Jesus came and stood among them and said, "Peace be with you." [John 20.19,20; NRSV]

Foreheads and Ritual

HE HAD FALLEN OUT with the previous pastor and left the Church. Now he was dying and his wife came to me to see if I would bring him communion, if I would reclaim him for God, I think. I visited him in hospital. He was now too frail to get out of bed and I shared communion with him and his wife. When we had finished the Eucharist, I anointed him with oil, making a cross on his forehead.

It was as if I'd hit the start button on a tape recorder! He began to recount all the Ash Wednesdays he had attended, and no doubt the infant baptism that was beyond his memory. In that physical, ritual act, a memory bank of belonging was triggered and he rested in his membership in Christ. He died a few days later.

It leads me to ask if we plant the peace of our passing in the rituals we live out in church all the time–communion, baptism, Ash Wednesday, prayers and anointing. Do we lay up treasures in our repetitive ritual that is cashed in as we move out of earthly life into God's presence, however and whenever that occurs? Could it be that these habitual acts are like our insurance when we are ill unto death and unable to meet with the faith community as we have in times of health?

> ...*you are dust, and to dust you shall return*
> *[Gen.3.19; NRSV]*

Forgiveness and Peace

I WONDER IF YOU'VE ever received forgiveness from someone in a deeply personal way, not just for squeezing the toothpaste the wrong way, but profoundly, in the furthest depth of your being. Do you recall first of all having to acknowledge your own need for forgiveness, and the pain and fear of needing to say, "I'm sorry; please forgive me?" And the dread of what your confession of wrongdoing might cost? Are you blessed to remember the liberation and relief you felt when someone significant forgave you when they might have reacted otherwise? Receiving forgiveness of this magnitude releases peace into our lives, peace and a lightness of living freely.

A number of realities inhibit this process in our contemporary, cultural approach to life. Firstly, we are beset by our unwillingness to admit wrong and therefore to confess a need for forgiveness in the first place. We are much more inclined to assign wrong to others in an attempt to absolve ourselves of any culpability. Secondly, we don't want to submit ourselves to each other's assessment and risk judgment or outright rejection.

If doing this inter-personally is difficult, imagine how difficult it is to recognize, and take ownership of, our personal brokenness before our creator and then accept God's solution and provision for our need for forgiveness. The design of the atonement is to say that we can give up all responsibility for our failure to God who forgives us and offers us absolution for our shortcomings and our, dare I say it, sins. This is the great design of Christian faith. We must recognize that we are broken, that we need repair, that we must confess that reality, and that God has provided a means by which we can be forgiven and experience peace.

So, what does this have to do with end of life questions? One of the pressing realities, as we come to the end of our earthly time, is the question of how we will be judged for how we have lived our lives. It seems to me that, if we can face death with a profound sense of peace, resulting from our experience of forgiveness, then we will enter into that final experience of death prepared for the future God has always planned for us.

So it turns out that the Atonement is actually the central element in a healthy life and a healthy death.

> Be kind and compassionate to one another, forgiving each other, just as in Christ God forgave you. [Eph.4.32; NIV]

Funerals

IN AN IRISH FILM comedy called "Waking Ned Divine," one of the main characters of the story attends his own funeral. I don't want to disclose the plot, so let me just say that the humorous circumstances of the film made it possible for one character to hear his best friend eulogize him in the service. Afterwards, he expressed his amazement to his friend that he had thought all of those kind things about him at all.

It's true, isn't it, that all of the things that people say they appreciated about the dead person are said when they are gone and go unheard by the deceased; at least, we have no proof that they do hear what is said about them. I have presided at many funerals, and even eulogized my own mother and father, and I reflect that words and feelings are shared that should better have been said to the one no longer alive.

I suppose I'm suggesting that we take less for granted in our earthly relationships, and we should weigh what we value about each other and share it as appropriate. We can never be sure that the opportunity to do so will always be available to us. Perhaps, telling each other what we appreciate about them might be the beginning of a more redemptive and caring community.

> *I thank God every time I remember you, constantly praying with joy in every one of my prayers for all of you . . . [Phil.1.3; NRSV]*

Future Perfect

. . . the resurrection of the dead and life everlasting

IT'S INTERESTING THAT THE words that end the Creed at the same
time actually point us forward into our future with God. It's a future that has been guaranteed for us in Christ's resurrection and
ascension, the first fruit of God's redemptive plan for all creation.
It's somewhat curious that the chronological form of the Creed
places the most important truth as the last utterance. After all, it is
in the resurrection of Christ that all meaning resides; without that,
there would be no Christian faith, no church per se and certainly
no creeds. It is what sets us apart.

So many more people seem inclined to bask in the glow of the
Incarnation than are content to embrace the power of the Resurrection and its significance. I wonder why that is so! The miracle
of each is similar, with heaven touching earth in wonderful and su-
pernatural ways. Without the truth of the Resurrection, however,
there would be no reason to celebrate the obscure, ancient birth
of a Jewish baby in dubious circumstances, impoverished and of
unclear parentage. It is only that the child became the man Jesus,
and walked among the people of Israel, healing, preaching and
announcing the coming of the Kingdom of Heaven, that makes
us take note. Even those years of ministry would have dimmed
into history where it not for the Passion, Resurrection and Ascension. All meaning in Creation was poured into that act of God,
on the cross and in the tomb, and all meaning flows out of it into
our lives bringing meaning, purpose and future. We fail to affirm

the resurrection of the dead and the cost is a faith ill-founded and useless.

I suppose it could be our reticence to think of our own deaths, or our human limits, that displaces the Resurrection as the central tenet of Christian faith. Not many of us speak familiarly of our mortality; even those who have faced death find it difficult to talk about. And I'm not trying to suggest we should embrace death or revel in it; rather we should embrace a future with God that includes death but also "life everlasting," in a new heaven and a new earth. That, after all, is how the Creed ends, with the "future perfect." Insofar as the Kingdom of Heaven has already been inaugurated in Christ, I believe our walk of faith should give us occasional glimpses into that abundant, everlasting life that God wants for us. From time to time, as we seek God's face, informed by the whole of the Creed, we can see the future now. Perhaps it is in the face of a special loved one, or the birth of a new baby, or the glory of creation; but sometimes, we see what God wants for us and for all of creation. Maybe you have experienced moments when you could feel the warmth of God's embrace, and the knowledge that you are deeply loved by the one who formed you. That's what gives you a glimpse of your perfect future. Unfortunately, our lives are beset with busyness and distraction so much that we do not often take time to watch for the glimpses of heaven we might get if we intentionally open up our eyes and see.

An image that has helped me to appreciate the glimpses we sometimes get comes from experiences at our cottage by the lake. I particularly enjoy thunder and lightning storms at night, and have been known to go down to the dock in the rain and dark. In the blinding flashes of lightning, the whole lake is momentarily illuminated as if it were daylight, and I can see the far shores of the lake as clearly as ever. It doesn't last long, of course, but it assures me that the shore is still there and all is well in spite of the storm and the dark. For me, the Christian life is a lot like that experience. It is full of storms and struggle and sometimes I wonder about the state of things and what the future will bring. Occasionally, though, God shines through into my life just like the lightning and

I know all is well–the future is in place in spite of the present! I need to "bank" those glimpses and rely on them for my sense of hope and peace. All meaning flows into the Resurrection of Jesus, and all meaning in life and our eternity flows out of it. That is why, for me, the end of the Creed is its most important part:

I believe in the resurrection of the dead, and life everlasting.

> *Then beginning with Moses and all the Prophets, Jesus interpreted to them the things about himself in all the scriptures. [Lk.24.27: NRSV]*

G.

Grace

I'VE ALWAYS FOUND THE phrase "God's riches at Christ's expense" a helpful way of understanding, simplistically I'm sure, the idea of "grace." Because of God's initiative in the sending of Jesus into history, a redemptive option was made available to the human creature, an option designed to lead to a life more abundant and fulfilled, a life forgiven and purposeful. On most days, I do feel that my life is better because of belief, and that Christ's sacrifice has freed me from the inevitable end of brokenness, and yes, sin.

The final reckoning or test of this awareness is still to come, and as I approach the end of earthly life, I recognize that only behind the curtain of death will I be sure of what I say I believe now. Having said that, I take some comfort in my conviction, shared I think with the Apostle Paul, that the transition from life to "new life" will be quite seamless, even though the "curtain" between now and then seems as fixed and dark as a moonless night in the depth of winter.

These are heady questions to be considering, I suppose, but surely people of faith are supposed to look ahead and to weigh the promise of faith that in eternity awaits them, and that that's a good thing!

Through Jesus Christ our Lord, [we] have received grace and Apostleship to bring about the obedience of faith for the sake of his name among all the nations ....
[Rom.1.5; ESV]

H.

Heart attack

IT'S OVER TWENTY YEARS since a cardiologist sat on my hospital bed and asked if I had any family history of heart disease. At that point, I answered him with a "No, not as far as I know." Now the answer would be dramatically different. Not long after my attack, my mother dropped dead of a heart attack, albeit in advanced years. Subsequently, I've discovered that her brother, my uncle, died at forty-two of his third heart attack and his son, my cousin, had already had his first attack by the age of forty. I now had a family history that I'd never known about! My own heart disease has been carefully monitored and medicated over the years and I guess I have so far beaten the family odds, on my mother's side at least.

I can still vividly remember that first hospital bed after I had experienced difficulty and my kind of stunned disbelief at what had happened; my personal journey with my mortality and finitude began in that experience. I no longer carry the anxiety that my heart could fail at any moment but I'm fairly sure how my end will finally come–barring an accident or some such thing. Apart from being careful, there is little more to do about it.

I suppose it's good to remember that and to revisit the mortality reality reflectively and prayerfully now that I'm soon to pass the post in my allotted lifespan.

Who can live and never see death? [Ps.89.48; NRSV]

Heaven

I'VE NEVER HAD A good sense of what heaven or paradise might look like, and honestly, never longed to go there. Apart from one woman's description of her husband's post-death destination [Cf. fear, 30 ff.] there's never been a visual image in my mind. The symbolic language of scripture has also never left me with a sense of longing for that as a destination.

I recently rediscovered a little booklet written by Joseph Bayley called, Heaven. It's illustrated by the calligraphy of Tim Botts and is eye-catching and beautiful. More importantly, it helped me reconsider my life after its earthly portion. While it acknowledges that the "death incident" may cause pain, as we may have experienced pain in the passage called birth, it points to the wonderful destination called Heaven.

Bayley puts into God's voice the concern that nothing written has managed to describe the reality of the after-life, any more than "a pineapple" could be described by a "tundra Eskimo." The picture that is given is one of a life of maturity and giftedness in which we'll be able to produce arias or poems, carve wood or paint landscapes, or especially for my wife, plant gardens "without sweat, drought or weeds."

I'm so glad for Bayley's vision of a heaven of productivity and creativity, not in the least passive or bland. There will be justice and relationship with the persecuted on earth, and the absence of guns, violence and wars.

I still want to avoid death, but heaven is now much more palatable. For that I'm thankful.

Rejoice and be glad, for your reward is great in heaven.
[Matt. 5.12: ESV]

Heritage

I BELIEVE THAT ONE's heritage, family of origin, shapes you in powerful ways, sometimes good and perhaps sometimes bad. Before he died, my father wrote a bit of an autobiography which I've found very helpful in sorting out some of my history and heritage. Mind you, in the deepest issues that I would want to know more about–such as the birth death of my older brother–my father did not reveal the depths of his pain or how he dealt with it. How, for instance, did it effect his pastoral work? Did he have deeply held questions about the nature of God because of that loss? I must assume that there were unresolved things that were his burden alone.

It's clear that most of the values that drove both of my parents are values that I hold and honour–honesty, loyalty, service and support of others, faith, intelligence, learning for example. These are important elements of my heritage, I'm convinced.

Of course, both of my parents had damage from their respective families of origin. I don't believe my father was ever freed emotionally as a person; a hyper-nervous, manipulative mother and a father that was somewhat weak, however nice he was, meant that my father was more limited in his emotional responses than was ideal. My mother had lost both parents and a younger sister by the age of eight or nine; she had seen her two brothers sent to another part of the family and country, while she went to an aunt and uncle where she suffered sexual abuse. It reads like a novel worthy of Dickens. Because of her own dissolved family of origin, my mother was fiercely dogged about protecting our little family–in fact, she found it extremely difficult to release me into adulthood at all.

It's obvious, on that side of the ledger, that I have influential heritage as well; it left me initially repressed (a tight religious context was part of that also) and anxious, and not able at first to stand on my own feet in the world. To step out of that past has taken more effort than I would wish another time.

So, I have regrets at this stage of life that I didn't grow up sooner. Having said that, I do recognize the riches of my heritage, and can even now thank my parents for doing so much with what life dealt them.

> *Honour your father and your mother, so that your days may be long in the land that the Lord your God is giving you. [Ex.20.12; NRSV]*

Home

As an immigrant child of an itinerant pastor, my idea of "home" was an elusive and somewhat remote concept. I've since observed with some personal envy my spouse, who is from quite a large family and has a strong sense of home as a place, together with her parents now gone and her siblings. There is a concreteness of home to her that seems to have come from the long-term stability of knowing where that home was located. For me, there has never been that kind of certainty; at best, home meant relationship with my parents wherever that was geographically at the time.

I suppose that I'm ahead of the game in not being attached to home as a specific place; Christians are after all meant to be pilgrims on a journey, a journey that has an ultimate destination in the arms of God. To the extent that we live each day of our lives in God's purposes, we're already "home" where we belong, even in the here and now. It is all, however, a promise of the time when we'll be truly home with God and not contaminated with the struggle we face in life to honour our true purpose rather than being defined by the culture's ends.

> Trust me. There is plenty of room for you in my Father's home. If that weren't so, would I have told you that I'm on my way to get a room ready for you? [John 14.2; The Message]

I.

Icon

IN MY FIRST PASTORAL setting, I developed a friendship with an elderly man toward the end of his life; in fact, he did die in my time with him. In our talks about the spiritual life, he told me once of a discipline he had. His practice involved looking each day for cross-shaped images, icons I might suggest, whereby he could be reminded of the Cross, and its place in his life. Bob was a remarkable man who had lived his life in the advertising business. It was a great lesson for me, early in my pastoral work, to realize that Godly people are in all walks of life - and that that's God's plan.

WHEREVER WE ARE, OUR responsibility is to practise our faith as if we were a beacon for others.

I grew up in a very Protestant home where images and icons were considered "far too Catholic to be good." Thankfully as an adult I have grown up to appreciate God's activity in a wide variety of places and people. I've found myself attracted to icons as "meaning-carriers for the faith." Bob's seeking out of cross images was a wonderfully disciplined way to live a day and to be reminded of the faith in one's heart. I have tried his faith discipline and been astounded by how often the "cross-shaped icon" appeared, and how easily it served as a reminder of whose I am. They say that's how fasting works: our hunger pangs are reminders to exercise our discipline of prayer. Fasting has never really worked in my life, but Bob's cross icon has.

ICON

For in him all the fullness of God was pleased to dwell, and through him God was pleased to reconcile to himself all things, whether on earth or in heaven, by making peace through the blood of his cross. [Col.1.20; NRSV]

Identity

As a young person, the shaping of my identity, my sense of who I was or who I would become was an agonizing thing. While I loved sports, and was even good enough to be on teams, it was clear that I could never aspire to being star material. In school, I was bright but undistinguished; teachers always told my parents that I had the ability to do so much more. I was short for much of my growing up years, and then merely average or even a little under-sized physically. What identity I could claim was that of the class clown, a convenient cover for my insecurity.

As I left for university, it was totally unclear to me who I was, or what I was to be. Through the next few years my identity was more shaped by what I was not to be than anything else. Inability to get into medical school was a significant disappointment, and many friends "moved on" when they got in, and I felt deserted by them. At the same time, I fell in love with the woman who is my partner to this day; but that did not really resolve my sense of identity automatically. After a Masters in English, three years of teaching high school, a year of film studies, and eight years of business in the film industry, I entered seminary to study for the Anglican priesthood. The whole of this journey was bathed in a kind of personal identity fog.

Parallel to the latter stage of this hazy advance was a developing sense of being a child of God. As my faith developed, this new identity also began to take shape. Most of life only confused me about my discovery of self, and events such as the death of my parents have only muddied those waters further. Now that I'm aging and in my senior years, nothing much of that identity I sought is very helpful at all. Of course, I have family of my own, children and grandchildren and I love them dearly–but I can't look to them as architects of my identity. I will leave them when I die; they have a certain passing quality. As a child of God, I have an eternal identity that will outlast the earthly and physical nature of this limited life. Can I approach death, not as a loss, but as a gain? I think that exploration holds promise.

> For it was you who formed my inward parts; you knit me together in my mother's womb. [Ps.139.13; NRSV]

Inevitability

THE DRAMATIST SAMUEL BECKETT once wrote starkly to describe the destiny of each human being:

> *Astride the grave, a difficult birth . . .*
>
> *In describing the human condition, this is the succinctly dark way Ibsen speaks of birth as the beginning of an inevitable journey to the grave.* [7]

While it's difficult in principle to argue against this extremely telescoped version of life, Christians want to see more. Entering the Reign of God, as those who believe in Christ would postulate, opens our lives to being lived abundantly as a celebration. Each day is to be lived fully without being palled by the inevitability of our limited lives. Not only that, but our participation in God's Reign opens up for us an eternal vista that far outlasts the grave and acknowledges the defeat of death, the antidote for the "sting" of death. Will Beckett's baby die? Absolutely! But in belief it will also live triumphantly up to and through death. Which inevitability will we serve?

> *For God has not destined us for wrath, but to obtain salvation through our Lord Jesus Christ, who died for us so that whether we are awake or asleep we might live with him.*
> *[1 Thess. 5.9: ESV]*

Inheritance

IF YOU'RE INTENT ON leaving an estate to a succeeding generation, it seems to me you're already living after your death. We do that, I'm sure, so that we will in some manner live on in the memories of those who follow us. The inheritance that we bestow on those we love who come later is a legacy that we give because of our love for those who inherit our wealth and chattels.

Isn't it interesting that God has also left believers an inheritance, one that will stretch unendingly into our future in a new heaven and a new earth? What we plan to leave to our own is perfectly acceptable while it is hard to imagine that God out of great love for us has left each of us an inheritance too. An eternal presence and relationship with our maker is our inheritance; we would do well to count on that as much as our own will count on our generosity.

> By his great mercy he has given us a new birth into a living hope through the resurrection of Jesus Christ from the dead, and into an inheritance that is imperishable, undefiled, and unfading, kept in heaven for you, who are being protected by the power of God through faith for a salvation ready to be revealed in the last time. [1 Peter 4; NRSV]

J.

Justice

ONE THING THAT SORELY restricts our ability to experience peace in life is our desire to see justice done, particularly in situations involving our own personal hurts. When life delivers instances in which we are abused or disregarded by others, we feel badly hurt and in the simplest words, want revenge and to see the injustice righted. Often, we can carry these wounds of injustice done to us for many years and sometimes to our graves. Theses scars can niggle and bother us; they can also affect our view of God whom we may think should have seen our damage and undone it.

This sense of injustice can be seen at both macro and micro levels in the human condition. I have observed partners in failed marriages unable to "move on" because of outrage about their treatment at the hands of the other. Sometimes, the system at least seems to promote economic injustice for one of the partners left behind, usually the woman. Being burdened by the revenge motive is made worse by the practical injustice of the circumstances after the marriage. Nevertheless, true health is not to be found on the track called "justice," only on the track called "forgiveness." This is a hard truth to appropriate, and for some it seems impossible.

Forgiveness is the only solution to larger injustices as well, injustices at a macro or socio-political level. I think of the atrocities of Rwanda and Hitler, and the evil of leaders like Amin in Uganda. As soon as we tie our sense of peace to the resolution of such immense problems, we doom ourselves to writhe endlessly in agony over the brokenness of the human condition.

In the Parable of the Wheat and the Weeds, Jesus clearly teaches that the resolution of injustice, in most instances, is to await the culmination of all history and the final reckoning by God, the only One equipped with all the facts and the weight of truth to bring to bear.

This is another instance of facing our end and having to trust that right will be victorious. It is our lot to let God be God and to live in the future justice of the Kingdom of Heaven, in which our citizenship is sure.

> ... *if you weed the thistles, you'll pull up the wheat, too. Let them grow together until harvest time.*
> *[Matt.13. 29,30: The Message].*

K.

Knowing

IT'S PRETTY CLEAR THAT "knowing things" is very important to me, as I believe it is for many in Western culture. A handful of degrees and my constant state of personal curiosity, together with the plethora of information sources available today, are strong indicators of that. On a billboard somewhere, I recently saw the adage that "knowledge is power!" In fact, knowing things has become a commodity in our society. It is now the focus of our technological age, if not its idol. The unfortunate reality is that there is much of importance in our lives that cannot be sublimated into knowledge. Never is that more apparent than at the time of death, and it is why we feel so powerless to understand what's happening to us.

The unknown, mediaeval mystic who wrote the spiritual classic, The Cloud of Unknowing, noted that our deep awareness of God relies first on our being emptied of all other perceived knowledge before we are able to be filled with the fullness of God. This stage in the spiritual life is known as "purgation" and is at odds with our contemporary culture that places such a premium on the quest for knowing. Being filled with information contrasts the emptying of knowledge and understanding.

When it comes to matters of life and death, we find that we are essentially empty of any knowledge about the experience we must ultimately face. That is why we figuratively throw up our hands in despair, or avoid the issue all together. We just don't know anything! We know in our deepest selves that we are not in control and that scares us. All we have sought to discover comes up short and we are fearful.

Perhaps that is the greatest value of facing our human limits: we are finally able, if we choose, to be filled and overflowing with the knowledge of a God who loves us and embraces us in all our poverty of knowing. People achieve this status in differing degrees. Some discover much as they glimpse God's future, while others seem oblivious or lacking understanding.

Only death provides the complete emptying that allows God to reside with us. Those who seem to die at peace, as far as we can tell, embrace that final emptying in the knowledge that all emptiness will be absorbed into the love of the One who made us and who welcomes us.

> Let the same mind be in you that was in Christ Jesus who...
> emptied himself ... and became obedient to the point of
> death. [Phil.2.5-8; NRSV]

L.

Loved

AT THE HEART OF our personal sense of security and meaning is our awareness of being loved and being loved in a variety of ways. As children we yearn and absolutely need to be assured of our parents' steadfast love for us. Anything less and we inherit personal adjustments that can hound and limit us throughout our lives.

As adults we seek out the love of friends and partners. These love relationships enable us to take on the challenges of adult life. As we enter the world and try to succeed in our various enterprises, we rely on a secure home base where we can be sure of ourselves and confident of support and embrace. There, we can lick our wounds and be restored in order to enter the fray once again.

Parents and partners do not, however, answer all our needs for being loved. There is one deepest need that surpasses all others–that is our profound need to know we are loved by God. This love is experienced at our most personal and profound level of needing approval and belonging; it speaks to our sense of purpose; it also addresses our place in all creation. It's a love that surpasses all other loves and has a more profound purpose as well; it ultimately extends beyond time and space and transcends the limitations those realities place upon us in our earthly life.

I have to admit that this assurance of being loved by my maker was not something I came to easily. In spite of a faith-based home and upbringing, I was not assured of my "beloved by God status" until mid-life. What I possessed until then was an intellectual, or perhaps theological, affirmation of that love.

There were certain factors at work in this delayed confidence, I think, that worked against my celebration of being the beloved. My early years offered me a fairly repressed view of God and one that was framed in patriarchal terms. Not only that, but my sense of God was further limited by male and somewhat militaristic imagery. To some extent, God as Father limited my sense of being loved. For various reasons of upbringing and intellect, my father offered me a cool and intellectual form of love. To be fair, Dad was shaped by an emotionally diminished family of origin; it's not surprising that he was damaged, and I no longer blame him for that. It was not a love that I found emotionally convincing or that warmed me as a beloved son. Dad always tried to extract better results from me; in school, even if I achieved ninety-nine per cent, it was the one percent that concerned my father. Never being totally good enough is my memory of my father's expressed approval. My early conception of God was of a cosmic father and it was limited by my human experience. Now I know that to be the beloved is to be wonderfully good enough, just as I am.

It was my mother who was the warm and accepting centre of life for me. When my dog died–I was fourteen–it was my mother who absorbed my tears and anchored me to move on, in spite of my father's disapproval. It was only in later years, as I began to appreciate the fullness of God - transcending and fully incorporating maleness and femaleness - that I began to appreciate how much God loved me. It allowed me to incorporate my mother's breast as a site of love for me–there I knew I was the beloved of God.

To be assured of God's love, specifically to know that God has provided for my access to the Creator's bosom is to release me into a life of confident beloved-ness; it is this that allows me to live confidently at this late stage of life into whatever the future holds, come death or high water!

God is love and those who abide in love abide in God, and
God abides in them. [1 John 4.16; NRSV]

M.

Marriage

MARRIAGE AND FAMILY HAVE shaped much of what I have become at this point of my life. And much of the goodness of that is due to my life partner. Scripture talks of man and woman becoming one, and I can truly say that because of my partnership I have felt whole.

My wife is not perfect–and neither am I! So, don't think my idyllic description of our marriage is without difficulty or that it hasn't taken hard work and commitment from each of us. But mostly, it is right and good and God-blessed.

In fact, I've personally learned more about God in the context of family than I ever expected. On the best days, I know that I love my partner as much as I love myself. I look at my now adult children and can actualize how God loves me, with all my imperfections and warts and limitations.

Maybe most importantly, I have known and felt forgiveness in my marriage and glimpsed the God-forgiveness that is at the heart of grace. I've also learned that I can pass that forgiveness to others, even when they've hurt me. Through good times and difficult, my marriage has made me a better person and a better believer. One of the anxieties I experience when I think of dying is that it'll be the end of marriage. I hope God has sorted out a contingency plan for that!

MARRIAGE

Therefore a man shall leave his father and mother and hold fast to his wife, and they shall become one flesh.
[Gen.2.24;ESV]

Meaning

I remember quite vividly my thirtieth birthday and the weeks surrounding it. At that time, I was struggling futilely with my identity and purpose in life, demanding from God some guidance for my life and whatever vocation was to be mine. I do not remember this time with fondness, or the glow of miraculous insight and discernment. Rather there was mostly a sense of despair and gloom. As I look back on that period of life from my current viewpoint, I realize–at least on my good days!–that I was asking all the wrong questions about life's purpose and my own significance within that purpose

Ironically, the more senior, "wiser!!" years seem to bear similar issues–you'd think a life well lived would have meant some resolution or understanding of the meaning of life. Nevertheless, as professional roles devolve and as age creeps up on me, I find my current struggles have had some similar shapes to those of earlier years, albeit with a different tense. "How have I lived my life?" and "What did I really accomplish?" are questions that float through the ether of my mind from time to time; and they are damn hard to face sometimes. They are, of course, again the wrong questions to be asking.

Some twenty-eight weeks into her first pregnancy, my younger daughter developed severe health problems. It became clear that something was wrong with her pregnancy and she was hospitalized with high blood pressure and a condition known as "pre-eclampsia." This condition can be quite threatening to the life of fetus and mother, and it is connected to a flawed placenta. After monitoring her carefully, it became clear to the doctor late on a Saturday night, that a Caesarian section would be required and an exceptionally early birth, not what we had been praying for at all. A baby only twenty-eight weeks old is highly premature and at considerable survival risk. As it turned out, the premature delivery of the baby disclosed a separated placenta with no hope of future vitality; so, the right thing had been done. Thankfully the baby breathed on his own when birthed and proceeded to hold his own in Intensive Care; he weighed one pound, thirteen ounces–and was the tiniest infant I'd ever seen.

Very early on a Sunday morning, I found myself in the Neo-natal Intensive Care of Women's College Hospital, peering into an incubator at my grandson, as miniscule as he was. Everything seemed to be normal apart from his size, and of course some still developing and important internal functions. As I looked at him, God whispered to me that I shouldn't worry because this little one was just as loved by God as even I was. With little to commend him - no apparent vocation, no professional title or role, no ac-complishment, not even a voice–and yet, as much as it was true for me, God held this little one in His arms and expected no more of him than to be his beloved. That's what life was about: to recognize God's love and be held up by it. This, after all, was what Christ's atoning work made available to us. Everything else in life flows from that. Whatever was to happen, my grandson had it made already!!

We live in a culture that confuses us all the time and deflects us from this incredibly simple starting point for our meaning in life: that is that we are loved and held in a firm embrace by our Cre-ator. If we just get that right and let that truth's significance sink in, all the other stuff will settle out properly. This is an understanding that the culture of acquisition tries to erase. This culture tries to tell us, in thousands of ways, that we still don't have the right "stuff," and we must keep trying to gain acceptance and to acquire the proof of that. We can also be tempted to acquire accomplishments, and thereby status and influence. This is the risk of the working life in which we are urged to strive for success and achievement, whether it is that next step up the corporate ladder, or the next book published, and so on. In all of these subtle challenges, we are often most intrigued by our own potential Messiah status and try to become the center of the universe and its meaning.

Looking at my grandson, even in all his vulnerability, reminded me that it is only in relationship with our Creator that true meaning lies. At our most empty, we are as full as we need to be to receive God's love and promise. To appreciate that is to know what life's about, whether you're thirty or seventy, or just twenty-eight weeks old. To live in that relationship is the meaning of life; it enlivens our living and it cushions our dying. Thanks be to God.

> *. . . the time came for her to deliver her child. And she gave birth to her firstborn son and wrapped him in bands of cloth, and laid him in a manger. [Luke 2.6-7; NRSV]*

N.

Nearer my God

IN THE MID-19TH CENTURY, Sarah Flower Adams wrote a hymn of piety and evangelical intensity called "Nearer my God to Thee." On the night of April 15, 1912, that hymn took on a whole new identity as the music that was played and heard as the mighty ship, Titanic, sank into the North Atlantic. Much has been made of the band members who played to the end and sacrificed their lives in the tragedy. Their assignment, when the dire circumstances of the voyage were known by those in charge of the ship, was to play in the first class lounge to keep spirits up. They had finished their actual shift and re-gathered to give comfort to those passengers who were suddenly scared about their lives and whether they were to survive on this "unsinkable leviathan."

By the time it became clear to all of them, that the great ship was "going down," the band had moved outside to the forecourt deck aware that the stakes had been significantly increased. It was then that they turned to the playing of "Nearer my God to Thee." Even those who were to survive in the frigid waters of the North Atlantic could hear the faint streams of the hymn wafting from the deck of the sinking vessel.

For many in our contemporary culture, there's little thought of destiny in the frenetic pace of day-to-day life as we experience it. Only when the spectre of death arises do we turn our minds to what may lie ahead for us, after we die. It's then we want to be assured of the presence of our creator and a future and ongoing relationship with the One who has made us. Unfortunately, that immediately assumes that God is part of our death and not necessarily an active participant in our lives here on earth. The fact that we sing about God's nearness when we face death, albeit true, fails to account for the vitality of relationship that God desires with us in the reality of our daily lives. Yes, God is there in death and beyond, but also and maybe more immediately important, God is with us in the here and now.

> Truly I tell you, today you will be with me in Paradise.
> [Luke 23.43; NRSV]

O.

Obituaries

IN ALL MY LIFE I've never read obituaries. Now my local newspaper has dedicated a whole page to obituaries of people who led "significant" lives; like it or not, death has sidled its way into my awareness. Something I've noticed about obituaries is that they feature lives of meaning. They only last a few paragraphs, and are there one day only, and are usually never seen again. They attempt to document the highlights of a life, but never help me think about or resolve my own death. What did these "significant" individuals think about their own pending passing? For all they accomplished in their interesting lives, not a jot or tittle of it helps me with my mortality, my limitedness! Did any of them have insights about their "creature-liness" that could help me process my end? I don't really care about the lives of the significant anymore unless they can show me how to die.

> For everything there is a season, and a time for every matter under heaven: a time to be born and a time to die.
> [Eccles.3.1-2; ESV]

Only Four

AT A RECENT ALUMNI event, I sat across the table from an aging graduate of my seminary and overheard some of his conversation with an old friend. When it came time in the programme to honour older graduates who had died in the past year, he said to his conversation partner, "there're only four of us left now." He said this with such poignancy and sadness that it caused me to reflect on the realities he was facing in his advanced years. He was, of course, referring to those men he graduated with decades earlier as they entered eagerly into a vocation of ordained ministry. Out of the twenty or so colleagues, all but four had died.

Trying to imagine the inner circumstances of this graduate, probably a couple of decades older than myself, I began to think about the feelings he must have had, and the feelings I could face where I to be alive that long myself. Even though his aged wife was beside him, I had a sense of his profound loneliness as he thought about that group of friends who would truly have understood his life and its pressures, but with whom he could no longer talk. He could no longer feel their support either, or just the knowledge they were on the same team. The players were no longer there in the same way. The sense of community had diminished. Who was alive that could remember what it was like in their day? The world has changed from that time, and none of the younger folk could appreciate the pressures and joys of his time.

Add to these factors the clearly failing body that just creaked more every day and needed more extensive support, and you could see that hope for the future was a commodity very difficult to sustain without the faith that a promise was in place for something profoundly better that the reality of life as it had become.

The predominant reality of "waiting" takes on many faces at this stage of life. There is the sense that one is waiting for the moment of passing over, when the increasing limitations of this time and space reality are transformed into whatever and whenever future God has promised. Waiting for that moment does have some fear of the unknown attached to it and inevitably is a little fearful. It also focuses the individual on the future that is waiting, and that focus can destructively demean the present and living as fully as possible in the reality of the here and now. Imagining what God has planned can detract from the meaning and value of the present.

So it seems to me it's a balancing act: live as fully as is possible in the present, but take comfort in God's future for you. The fact that only four are left from your graduating class has no value apart from statistics. Your work is to find the balance of a faithful life; that is to live as abundantly and thankfully as possible in the now while celebrating that there is also a "to come" to await eagerly. The timing is up to God.

> . . . *let us run with endurance the race that is set before us*
> *[Heb. 12.1; ESV]*

P.

Persistence

OUR DAUGHTER MADE HER request for pierced ears when she was just six. Although this may seem commonplace in our culture now, we were pretty clear that it was something that did not belong in the ear of someone so young. After consultation, we told her that she had to wait until she was thirteen before we would allow her to have her ears pierced. I suppose we thought of the teen years as a more appropriate time for the development of her personal statement of fashion.

Well, our denial of her request began a long and serious effort from her–a campaign really - to change our minds. She never wavered from her goal, she never gave up; this was persistence personified. And to persistence she added impeccable research in an attempt to assure us of the harmlessness of the procedure and where she could have it done safely.

Over time her strategy developed to the point that she informed us that the piercing of her ears was actually a justice issue. After all, her friends were having it done, and it just wasn't fair that her old-fashioned parents were holding out! I remember it as being just exhausting! And although we held out for a remarkably long time, we finally capitulated and she had the ears done when she was ten. Not thirteen as we had originally decreed, but ten.

My daughter's dogged perseverance has always been a bit of a model for me of the way we should live out our lives. Even in the so-called golden years, when we are sometimes tempted to "take time off," our task is to continue our journey with goals in mind. People of faith do this in the recognition that the journey "home" is not finished until the end of the race; even the last few yards require our supreme effort. We must persist in becoming all we're meant to become and not give up!

O, that my steps might be steady, keeping to the course you set. [Ps.119.5; The Message]

Perspective

WHY DO I FIND it so difficult to set time aside to develop my spiritual life? It just seems strange that something I know in my head to be critical to my wholeness and humanity is so hard to make a priority. For years, I worked in a theological college that was preparing people for Christian ministry; the hectic pace of life there always seemed to work against the deep spiritual growth that I believe God invites us into, especially as leaders. However important it is, theological "thinking" is not synonymous with theological "being." We can work extremely hard at understanding the faith intellectually, but fail sometimes to practice it personally and intimately.

Each year I organized a retreat for the graduating class of ordinands and accompanied them on their time away. We set this time apart early in the school term to be sure we couldn't weasel out of it when the day came and finishing assignments seemed to be the more important agenda. I personally always found those days deeply regenerative and spiritually stimulating. We always went to L'Arche Daybreak and were led in the day by the chaplain who is on staff there. The real work of the Spirit, though, was the encounter with the "core members" of the community, the people for whom the community exists. These L'Arche communities are all over the world now. The movement was founded by Jean Vanier in France and is now in over 130 countries. They offer the experience of "home" to people that often suffer with multiple handicaps and require significant care. Daybreak was also the home of Henri Nouwen before he died, and he wrote movingly of the transforming experience of caring for such individuals. Whether it is through the caring work of the assistants, often young students from around the world, or whether it is through the simple statement of the gospel by core members, it is clear that God's love is at work.

In the glow of God's love that shines so brightly through the ones Vanier called "wounded," our own attempts to prove ourselves worthy seem deeply tarnished by comparison. Core members live in the conviction that they are beloved by God and that they have a calling to be hospitable to all comers. They are so sure themselves of Jesus' love that they glow with the news of the gospel. I'm convinced that any of our Christian ministries must begin with the recognition of our own profound need and vulnerability. It is to that need that God directs grace through Christ. We spend so much of our time trying to prove to the church or parishioners or family that we are worthy of praise, that we forget there is only One truly worthy of praise. The broken-down core members of L'Arche are often so broken that no pretense is possible. It is precisely that truth that frees God's great love to do its healing and redeeming work. When one of those wounded ones stutters out the declaration that God loves him or her, the whole of the gospel is encapsulated in those words. There is no more to be said really.

It was good to have those days away in a place like L'Arche, and to be reminded that God loves me, just for who I am as God's creature, not for what I think, say or do. I am to rest in that knowledge as a beloved one and be thankful. As I catapult through my three score and ten years' allotment, perhaps I should revisit L'Arche and reclaim some of the perspective I always gained there in previous encounters with the core members of that community.

> For I am convinced that neither death, nor life, nor angels,
> nor rulers, nor things present, nor things to come, nor pow-
> ers, nor height, nor depth, nor anything else in all creation,
> will be able to separate us from the love of God in Christ
> Jesus our Lord. [Rom.8.38-39; NRSV]

Picking Peonies

IT'S EARLY SUNDAY MORNING and I'm watching my wife gather a bunch of flowers for her mother. She carefully collects the peony blooms into a posy of sorts and sets out on the journey to visit her mom. Her mother, my mother-in-law, is in her early nineties and in a long-term care home where her Alzheimer's disease progresses slowly but inevitably to its end. There are times when we wish her mom's life would end, and then we feel guilty for feeling that way; but the extent of that illness reaches out to include a whole family network. It is a sentence for all of us waiting passively in the light of increasing ill health and eventual death.

My wife and her sister each visit twice a week, and strive to care dutifully to the degree that's possible at this point. And so, the peonies, and a refusal to succumb to the life-sucking negativity of their mother's sickness, their mother's protracted dying.

I am humbled by their caring and dedication in the light of such a shadow over life. I suppose it's a way to live in promise, a promise of resurrection and repair ultimately. And so the flowers adorn the window sill in that "less than home" room as a loud declaration that, in spite of Alzheimer's, one day all will be well, and all will be well.

Consider the lilies how they grow . . . [Luke 12.27; ESV]

Promise in the fall

OF ALL THE SEASONS, I think the fall is my favourite. Gone are the humid and hot days of August when I seek out shade and air-conditioned space for protection. Autumn temperatures are more moderate and I don't need to hide out from the weather. It's also the time for harvest and a gathering of the garden's bounty; there's nothing like picking your own tomatoes and even the last of the ever-bearing raspberries. In the natural world, there's an industry about the season–migration has changed the outdoors' personnel, winter shelters are being stocked by little creatures with nuts and other foodstuffs, and then there's the general tidying up of the yard by the two-legged variety.

Most of all, I find Fall meaningful as a symbol of a much broader truth in that it points ahead to a another renewing of the cycle of the year. Although leaves are falling and the earth is sleepy, the future of another year's cycle is assured by the developing dormancy of this season. The seeds that bury themselves in autumn are the promise of new life to come.

This is also how I understand the Christian life, beginning with Christ and extending to us as well. Life, death and new life is the rhythm of faith for each one of us. New growth in the natural world depends in some measure upon a dying and being buried so that rebirth can result, in its right season. Observing my Christian experience from my "more senior than many" vantage-point, I've lived through many "life-death-new life" cycles and watched others experience the same reality. The growth from such cycles in life is important to us as Christians and allows us to face even the most difficult experiences with a sense of hope. That's why I've always said that the Christian agenda is to watch alertly for "good news" even in the midst of bad.

It is true for all of us that there is a seasonal reality to our lives. Not only have I experienced the renewing cycle many times before, toward the end of my life I can sense the coming of Fall colours personally. The challenge is to see the end of life in a larger perspective and with more promise than I must admit I sometimes do. Even at the moment of my final earthly breath, new growth of some kind is just around the corner of my year because I serve a God whose very nature is that of Creator and of new possibilities. My challenge in this struggle with mortality is to keep the faith and wait actively on the Lord for what is promised and near.

> *Unless a grain of wheat falls into the earth and dies, it remains just a single grain; but if it dies it bears much fruit. [John 12.24; NRSV]*

Prophetic children

It was an interrupted family Christmas at the cottage. In previous weeks, the wife's grandmother, the family matriarch, had died following a protracted illness and much care. Although sad, there was some relief and at the same time hope that she could now spend more time with her own mother, time that had been lost in the care of the matriarch. Into that family Christmas, came the news that the wife's mother had just died suddenly. Now the family was driving back to face another cycle of grief and loss. One can only imagine the wife's feelings as she faced that cycle with the added sense of lost potential and being robbed of a greater relationship with her own mother.

The kids were in the back seat, a boy of nine and a little girl of seven. As they headed back to the city, the young girl wrote and then passed this note to her mother. I'll include this from my memory retaining the features I remember:

> *Dear Mumy*
> *Its hard when mummies and grammas die*
> *but gramma is in heaven now and is moving toward the light.*
> *Shes sitting there now on the knee of God.*

Can children speak prophetically? I don't doubt it. This note of condolence passed to her grieving mother showed both wisdom and pastoral concern. Watch for children in human circumstances for they can sometimes be God's Voice to us, if we pay attention to them. In many ways children seem closer to God and less "fenced off" from the Almighty than we are.

In funerals particularly, children can be extremely impor-tant–to represent continuance, if nothing else. Or simply to offer a prayer in the liturgy, as did this same little girl in the funeral liturgy that followed.

Unless you accept God's kingdom in the simplicity of a child, you'll never get in. [Mark 10.15; The Message]

R.

Restoration

ONE OF THE JOBS I've always enjoyed is the restoration of old furniture, particularly "Canadiana" antiques. I don't do that nearly as much at this stage of my life, but I still sometimes find myself at it again. Actually, as we slowly get our adult children to reclaim their belongings, so we uncover projects still undone in closets and in the garage!

The process of antique restoration is actually quite challenging–it generally involves the removal of layers and layers of old paint, the repair of the wood surface and renewal of structural and working parts. Finally, there's the careful application of new finish, coat upon coat. The transformation is often quite dramatic, but it takes a lot of patient, hard work. And I confess that it's much more difficult and less appealing now than when I was thirty. Maybe it's just that my patience quota is lowering with age; I want gratification more quickly now!

I've often thought there are ways in which refinishing old furniture is a good metaphor for the reality of the Christian life. Of course, in this metaphor, God is the refinisher and I'm the furniture; but it often feels as if I'm experiencing the effort of the work, especially as I look ahead to possible renewal and transformation. The Christian life is harder work that I sometimes want to undertake; I think I can shy away from that effort and suffer a less significant life of faith than I should experience.

I realize that as I share my faith with others as an evangelist, it's important that I not "sell" the faith without admitting to the struggle required. New Christians can be shocked into inactivity by the difficulty of the Christian life when they had been told in a variety of ways that it was going to be "smooth sailing." Nothing in our world that claims to make life more fulfilling, and the Reign of God a reality, can go without challenge by evil powers.

I think the text that mandates our "refinishing" efforts is in Romans 12.2:

> Do not be conformed to this world, but be transformed by the renewing of your minds, so that you may discern what is the will of God–what is good and acceptable and perfect.

And so I return to the metaphor of refinishing old furniture, because renewing involves stripping away the layers of culturally coated accretions that can obscure and hide the beauty of my original wood. Like peeling back the layers of an onion, I need to get to the core truth of myself as a created being in relationship to my creator. It is only then that I can be enhanced and finished to show off, in all my beauty, what God desires me to become. Then, I can be a sign to our world of all God is about in the restoration of creation, the mission in which I share.

Maybe the idea of restoration could be applied to my struggle with aging. If aging is really improving me to become more and more regenerated, then thinking of my life in decline is probably looking in the wrong direction!

> Looking unto Jesus the author and finisher of our faith. . .[Hebrews 12.2; KJV]

S.

Small Stuff

IN A BOOKSTORE THE other day, I came across a book on the Self-help shelf that I thought might be worth thinking about. It was titled, Don't Sweat the Small Stuff, and the sub-title was "It's All Small Stuff!" I'm afraid I didn't take the time to explore the writer's wisdom, but I've thought a lot about the gist of the title.

It's true that there is a sense in the aging process, as personal demands lessen, that there is less to preoccupy us, less that feels urgent and important. The family, while always giving cause for thought and prayer, are largely on their own; and work respon- sibilities have either grown small or disappeared altogether. The things that filled our minds and days, and seemed to be so urgent, no longer have the same precedence.

Ideally, that should give us the opportunity to work through the big issues in life. By not "sweating the small stuff," we can pro- cess the most important things in our lives–ideally anyway!

Some time ago, I came across an editorial in our local paper in which a man turning seventy was reflecting on the things he needed to sort out before he died. He realized he no longer felt he needed to learn how to swim, and singing lessons weren't on his list any longer; but, he had decided that he needed to be clear about whether or not he believed in God. Since he had been an active churchman, albeit an Anglican like me, it was strange to read his confession about his lack of clarity on this matter. For all the Church duties he had undertaken–the small stuff I suppose–he still had not truly sorted out the most important question of all. It's easy to let the "small stuff" of life set our agenda, at the expense of the really important stuff. This time of life is given to us, perhaps, so that we can be really clear about what matters!

We love because he first loved us. [1 John 4.19; NRSV]

Suicide

ON A RETURN TRIP to Scotland, the country of my birth and that of my mother, we tried to find the burial place of one of her uncles in Perthshire. After searching through churchyards in the neighbourhood and failing to find his tomb stone, we finally visited the municipal cemetery. That's where we found his place of rest. As it turned out, he had committed suicide and his remains had not been allowed in a so-called sacred burial ground. It had to be the town ground for him. It is hard to account for such narrow and unfeeling a position about something which we see now as an illness like many others. The moment someone chooses to end life is a moment in which one is truly beside oneself, I believe. At another tragic funeral, I once heard Fr. Henri Nouwen say of the young man who had killed himself that he had lost the battle, but not the war. I found that a very helpful perspective. Let's rely on God's judgment about right and wrong, and not anticipate that by behaving in the way my great Uncle was judged.

In teaching a decade of ministers in training, I'd always taught them to prepare in advance for two extremely difficult funerals, that of a child and that of a person who has killed herself. In my first parish ministry, even though it was in a church full of young families, I never had to deal with the former tragedy. The same was true about a suicide.

Shortly after I left the parish, however, a doctor that I had worked with in pastoral and palliative situations in the community took her life, and I was called because there was no permanent replacement for me in the parish at the time–and more importantly, she had written to me as she died asking me to do the funeral, with clear instructions for how it should be conducted! It was extremely difficult to hear her in that note telling me what had happened to her and that she had run out of courage. She left behind her husband and two teenage sons and it was difficult to appreciate fully the pain she experienced and the pain she inflicted by her action. The truth is that, for all the times I'd told students to be prepared for such funerals, I found myself at "square one" as I struggled to be present and helpful in this situation. It was a remarkable funeral that brought together the varied parts of her life. She was a palliative care doctor, a specialist known well at the cancer hospital downtown; she was a member of our faith community; she was active in her own local community, walking the dog and sharing caringly with her friends; and she was well known in the local hospice. This woman walked with many who died under her care. This all magnified the tragedy and loss. The funeral was large and brought together all the elements of her life. As we considered that life, a lot of us asked what clues we had missed. We also noted that she kept each part of her life at a distance from the reality with which she was struggling. We had not known just how deeply her own sister's death had affected her, or the developing weight and fatigue that we call "caregivers' syndrome."

In addition to caring for the family, I found myself struggling to understand and accept her actions. How could I give comfort that was authentic and true to the reality of such brokenness? What could I say? So, the work I had said to my students should be done in advance of such pastoral realities I needed to do in a short time frame between receiving her note and leading the funeral. I have always found Annie Dillard helpful in addressing death: "When we lose our innocence . . . when we start feeling the weight of the atmosphere and learn there's death in the pot, we take leave of our senses." (Pilgrim at Tinker Creek) I confessed to the gathered community that my friend's actions had made me feel beside myself and went on from that point to face up to the loss, to note that faith was important as a context for our futures, to face up to the pressures of people who work in palliative care and that they themselves should not take their circumstances lightly or alone either. I think in the end it was a helpful funeral and it resulted in another service a week later in the amphitheater of the downtown hospital which was requested by the chief of staff who had been at the original funeral and who had written me in response to it. I led this funeral, with all its personal torment, in the cold shadow of the Municipal burying ground where my great uncle's remains are buried in another land and at another time.

Because the Lord your God is a merciful God, he will neither abandon you or destroy you. [Deut. 4.31; NRSV]

T.

Temptation

WHEN OUR DAUGHTERS WERE quite young, during an under-duress trip to the Golden Arches, we had a discussion about whether or not the decorative greenery between the booths was real or not. The discussion was authoritatively closed by the assertion by one of them: "Of course they're not real; real plants have brown tips!" She was absolutely correct. Every plant in those planters was a clone of the others and all were perfectly green, from base to tip.

Now, I prefer to label my daughter a pragmatist rather than a cynic, based on a vast array of other data over the years. Actually though, she had made a profound observation about life, more profound than she realized at the time. That observation is to say that life is messy, and brown tips abound. All of life is troubled by the reality that brokenness and failure co-habit with the best of our lives, whether we want to admit that or not.

No matter how we strive to live holy and acceptable lives, we make mistakes and succumb to the temptations that surround and assault us. Surely, that's the inherent wisdom of the Lord's Prayer: "lead us not into temptation but deliver us from evil." While it is not our intention to be tempted, and we ask God not to inflict that upon us, nevertheless we recognize that evil is abroad and we will need to be delivered from it from time to time.

We can certainly stack the odds against ourselves by the choices we make and can increase our risks by the influences we

engage, but the underlying reality is that we must live with temptation, engage it and seek support in struggling against it.

I wish I could write that this battle is won in my life; however,
I am forced to rely on confession and forgiveness more times than
I want to admit. I think God understands the extent of our struggle
and is generally merciful. That is why Jesus came into our midst
and ultimately died for our brokenness. It is upon that redemptive
sacrifice that I rely.

> *The Jesus was led by the Spirit into the wilderness to be*
> *tempted by the devil …. [Matt. 4.1; NRSV]*

Tides

ONE OF THE CHARMS of time spent at the coast for me is the deep joy I feel in the presence of tides. It's not just the constant change of the shoreline or the renewed richness of the tidal pools; it's the very fact of the tides themselves. They are as natural to creation as breathing is to us. They just seem to happen autonomically, intrinsic to the very design of the world. It's as if the breathing of creation was originally set in motion at some time beyond our awareness and certainly not by us. It describes for us just where we fit in the world, doesn't it!

> *And God said, "Let the waters under the sky be gathered together into one place, and let the dry land appear."*
> *[Gen. 1.9; NRSV]*

Time and Space

ONE OF THE REASONS clergy say such unfortunate things at funerals is that all of us simply don't know how death, and life after death, works. That's because the time-space continuum in which we live and understand life becomes meaningless at the time of our death. What replaces it is so totally unknown to us that it makes us incoherent when we try and grapple with the meaning of what happens to us when we die. While we desire to give comfort to those who mourn, we can sometimes affirm things about which we have no certainty. When we say, "Now, Julie sees God face to face," we're expressing our ultimate faith rather than our certainty about her actual immediate circumstances. What we can affirm is our conviction of God's promise to us that we will see God face to face; what we cannot be clear about is when and how that promise is realized. And that is because our time–space clarity ceases to have meaning for those who die. We can affirm promise, but we cannot speak to process or timing; it's just beyond our understanding.

That does not mean the failure of faith, or of the extent of God's power; it's simply a statement of the limits with which we live as human creatures. Imagine that at death the terms of human realities no longer describe, or limit, our relationship to God. That relationship is defined in a way in which we cannot as human creatures grasp; that should not depress us or concern us. There is a real sense in which the adventure of eternity is enhanced by the knowledge that we cannot now describe what the future holds for us.

And this is what He has promised us, eternal life.
[2 John 25; NRSV]

Transcendence

MY WIFE AND I love to be with whales. Whenever we're at the ocean we try to encounter them–Newfoundland, Vancouver Island, Grand Manan Island and the Bay of Fundy, the St. Lawrence River and Brier Island in Nova Scotia. We've been with whales in all these places. We love the athletic playfulness of humpbacks; we've observed at first hand the dramatic mating rituals of the Right whales; and we've chased Orcas in a wolf pack off Vancouver Island; but the most awesome whales in my book are the Finbacks.

Let me see if I can come close to describing them! Finbacks, and I've been very close to them in the Bay of Fundy, are up to 75 feet in length and extremely fast swimmers. Their size is generally hidden–only a dorsal fin about a third of the way along their bodies, and usually only a small part of their back is visible above water. It's so easy to underestimate them–unless you're very close.

But I have seen them close–the length and breadth of them– like the width of a church and 80 tons each!! If the nose was against one wall in the backyard, the tail would be flopped over the other wall of the backyard!

I don't know why, but every time I'm near whales I want more of them –maybe it's that I share mammal-ness with them, or maybe it's their intelligence because they're sometimes just downright curious and playful. But no; I think it's really the majesty of these creatures that takes my breath away. I just want to stay and be in some kind of communion with them. If you were a total stranger to maritime realities–and maybe you are -- can you imagine the trouble I'd have to convince you of what I'd seen? How could I possibly describe to you the scale of those amazing creatures?

That's what the transcendence of God must be like; God is so far beyond our categories of understanding, so other, that we stutter wordlessly in our attempt to describe God. Remember that this is the creator that conceived of and formed all those whales that I can`t describe to you properly. It`s all just a bit much for us, isn`t it. Such a good idea that God came to us in more manageable form to redeem us into usefulness. But remember that the whales are out there and God is God!

> *. . . my awe at your words keeps me stable.*
> *[Ps.119.161; The Message]*

Trust

THE CHRISTIAN FAITH IS founded upon trust. If God is God, then we can rest comfortably in the knowledge that what God promises is trustworthy. The difficulties arise in our doubts, doubts about God's trustworthiness and concerns about what we can confidently believe. Nothing puts a knife-edge on our concern more than our recognition of our limits, and that we must at some point come to an end of our earthly allotment of years. But we have also worked hard to manufacture a kind of social veneer to help us avoid that reality.

We live in an age of cynicism and the primacy of the individual and we've recreated ourselves as the centre of all understanding because we have justly learned to distrust institutions, diplomacy and leaders. At the beginning of the last century we experienced a technological renaissance that has evolved to the point that individuals have remarkable power and information available to them. What began as the flowering of modernity has now become postmodern individualism. What we most trust now is ourselves, and our capacity to find out whatever we need to know about anything. For example, people turn to the internet as an authority in their lives with no surety of there being authentic information there.

Trust in God has devolved into believing and trusting only in ourselves. We can also use this relocation of our place in the universe to deny the reality of our mortality. In fact, there even exists a chain of Anti-aging shops as a concrete symbol of this reality of denial. The multi-billion dollar cosmetics industry in North America alone is also dedicated in a way to masking the truth of our humanity and its inability to last forever.

What we have done with trust is to remove it from our lives. If God is dead, then we are in a difficult spot when it comes to dealing healthily with dying. We have lost an important frame of reference for understanding ourselves and our limits–not just understanding them, but accepting and maybe even celebrating them!

> *The one who trusts in the Lord is secure.*
> *[Prov.29.25; NRSV]*

U.

Unexpected

AN OLD ADAGE ADVISES us to expect the unexpected. It is perhaps no more true than in the so called "golden years" than it is at any other stage of life. Whether it is in our own sometimes perilous journey with health, or the tumultuous circumstances of our children's lives, or perhaps the turn of events for each of us, life very rarely dishes up the predictable. Far from the unexpected, we relish the familiar and predictable; but what we glean from life is more often the unexpected.

If that is true–and it is often so in my experience–what are we to do with the unexpected in our lives? I suppose the obvious guidance is that we must be better prepared for the unexpected, a particular commodity of our God. Instead of fearing the negative possibility of the unexpected, should we not celebrate its potential, instead. Let me suggest some possible ways in which that might work. I don't suppose many of us can imagine being mentors for succeeding generations–but imagine the potential of appreciating our role differently, no longer as the prime movers perhaps, but rather as advisors and wise counsel. Or perhaps, in community settings, we could find our wisdom and advice as a functional asset in the issues of our time. Settling into this kind of identity gives a new optic to our lives, instead of seeing ourselves as stale and outdated. Would that not be how our creative maker would see us in the constant rejuvenation by the one who loves us and uses us in the grand narrative of redemption?

God is a surprise, God is a surprise! [children's song]

Uniqueness

I BELIEVE THAT WE are each created in the image of God at the same time as being totally individual expressions of that image. As beloved creatures, we are valued by God for exactly the unique expression of humanity that we possess. It is this that makes us lovable to our Maker in a way that no other human being is; we are blessed because God has ordained our uniqueness and affirmed it, not unlike parents who perceive and speak well of their children. They are offspring but totally unique expressions of the same genetic code.

It's striking to me that, rather than celebrating our uniqueness, so often we try to be the same as the next person, and to have whatever it is that our culture is currently promoting as meaningful. There is little acceptance of the blessedness of the beauty and unique purpose that actually distinguishes us from each other.

That God loves us may be the most difficult thing to accept in our lives because it seems to run counter to so much we encounter in life. Being raised with things to prove, and in a culture that tells us what we lack and must seek after in order to be good enough, all indicate that we're not yet good enough to be loved and blessed. I appreciate what Christian writers such as Henri Nouwen and Mary Jo Leddy have said about the importance of gratitude as a starting point in a life of faith. Each in their way have pointed to a God who loves them abundantly for who they are. When we are sure of that blessing, we're able to contemplate passing on a blessing to others. When we can do that, it will be marked by our own unique expression of faith and faithfulness.

Being assured of God's unique blessing makes the whole idea of eternity far more palatable in my mind as well. When I can get past the weight of feeling "not good enough," I can move out from under the suspended doom over my head that I call death. I, yes humble little me, am loved by God for who I am; to be sure, God is very likely to want to spend a lot more time with me.

As my Father has loved me, so I love you; abide in my love.
[John 15.9; NRSV]

W.

Washing feet

As I WRITE THIS, it's Holy Week and I'm reliving the Paschal cycle in my local, parish church. I've just returned from the Maundy Thursday liturgy which features the washing of the disciples' feet by Jesus. I was struck again by the power of the symbolism of that act of humble service as a mark of how we are to interact with each other, and not only as Christians, but as human beings.

When my younger daughter married, she insisted that the washing of feet be exchanged with her beloved as part of the liturgy. Thankfully, I was not responsible for overseeing the service, and was relieved of the decision about its appropriateness in a wedding liturgy; ultimately, something I had never seen done was allowed. It was stunning and so appropriate to the vows and commitments they made to each other before God that day.

As the rhythm of the Maundy Thursday liturgy unfolded, I was led to wonder whether the washing of each other's feet isn't so important to the Christian community that it needs to have a more prominent and consistent role in our worship. I know that washing your guests' feet is not now a cultural imperative as it was in New Testament times, but symbolically it could reshape how we engage each other in life and death.

> So if I, your Lord and Teacher, have washed your feet, you
> also ought to wash one another's feet. [John 13.14; NRSV]

Wisteria

AT THE CORNER OF our backyard deck, we have an old and mature wisteria bush. It is truly the plant version of a prehistoric creature that looks gaunt, barren and ancient for most of the year. In the spring, however, it metamorphoses into a remarkable and extravagant flowering plant that overwhelms us with graceful and drooping blossoms. It is in its flowering time that a breathtaking change occurs. If one didn't know what was coming, one would not believe the transformation that takes place before your eyes. It's a celebration of creativity.

As I've reflected on how the wisteria spends most of its year compared to how it flowers, I wonder if the difference between our daily lives and what we are to become at the end of it all is not as dramatic. The resurrection body is so far beyond what we experience in time and history that surely it will take our breath away with its beauty and transformational reality.

> For this slight momentary affliction is preparing us for an eternal weight of glory beyond all measure, because we look not at what can be seen but at what cannot be seen; for what can be seen is temporary, but what cannot be seen is eternal. [2 Cor. 4.17-18; NRSV]

Workaholism

WHEN I WAS A young boy, our family acquired a cocker spaniel puppy. I can well remember her trying to speed through the kitchen, unsuccessfully careening around the corner in order to move through into the hallway. Her toenails on the tile floor gave her no purchase and the result was a little dog going nowhere very fast at the expense of a lot of effort. It was quite comical at the time.

Now I watch many in our world looking exactly the same. To be honest, I've done my own share of going nowhere fast as well! Many of us have been driven by work and achievement and at the frenetic, hyped up speed of electronic connectors. The unfortunate truth is that meaning lies in another direction altogether. Workaholism implies that it is "doing" that provides a measure of our personal significance. Rather, it is in our status as a beloved one that we have value. That is separated from anything we might feel we achieve through our own doing. "Being" trumps "doing" every time.

For me, being a parent taught me this lesson although I've struggled to understand it as a child myself. I have two wonderful daughters who I love dearly; I love them just because they are who they are as my daughters. I don't always agree with what they do, or even how they face life sometimes; but that never changes my deep love for them. Their significance as my daughters lies in the fact that I love them for who they are, separate from what they may or may not achieve by doing things. I would never seek their meaning or significance in their daybooks, as full and as important as those might appear. It's just not where meaning lies. I hope they can learn that one for themselves.

> *Therefore, since we are justified by faith, we have peace with God through our Lord Jesus Christ, 2through whom we have obtained access to this grace in which we stand; and we boast in our hope of sharing the glory of God. [Rom. 5.1-2; NRSV]*

Worship

IN THE PROCESS OF guiding a group of church members toward a statement of their purpose as a community of faith, we came to naming "worship" as one of our shared activities. After a brief moment, one person showed some hesitation with affirming this aspect of church life. "I don't know; it's as if we have to bow down to something," she said. I believe that my response at the time was to tell her "absolutely; you've got it!" In that, I clearly erred. She saw as a problem the fundamental Christian posture I considered essential to a healthy perspective.

I've thought a lot about her response in succeeding years and have realized that this described a defining moment in our attempt to know how to live abundant lives. It's about knowing where the power really lies. This, of course, is a true challenge to modern sensibilities in which we perceive ourselves as the centre of meaning, and yes, power. To acknowledge the need in our lives for a power beyond ourselves seems to many an admittance of personal failure to be all we think we can become. To think this way is to succumb to the grand lie of our age. We are in need of God at the centre of our lives; any true knowledge of human circumstances can only reinforce that reality.

I wonder if this "lie" is not behind our fear of death, the final act in our earthly lives that is apparently beyond our control. If we spend our lives without any need for a God, then the point of dying, or our thoughts about that moment in advance, become an unarguable weight in the evidence for how we have lived our lives in disregard of our creature-liness.

If we have felt in control while we live, what have we to say about the moment that is apparently beyond our control. Better to rest in the knowledge of a caring Creator who will stick with us beyond time and space.

> O come, let us worship and bow down, let us kneel before the Lord, our Maker. [Ps.95.6; NRSV]

X.

Xanadu

NAMED FOR THE SUMMER palace of the great Kublai Khan and commemorated in the poem by Coleridge and as the home of Citizen Kane in that famous film, Xanadu has long been idealized as the perfect home filled with fantasy, pleasure and wealth. In a sense, it's a metaphor for the rest, comfort and security that we believe one's ideal home should provide. Of course, the reality of homes can be quite different from individual to individual; they are sometimes very troubled and troubling places. The fantasy of a Xanadu is really just that, an elusive and inappropriate dream. It does lead us, though, to wonder just what is reasonable to expect of "home."

As one ages, one realizes that "home" is an evolving reality and never static. For many good reasons, we no longer visit our own childhood homes: distance, sold property, and as we grow older it's likely that our parents have died. What we know of the home in which we raised a family has also likely changed; children have probably grown up, left home and established their own families. As tempting as we might find it to remember the golden age of our family life, there is no way to make that any more than a fleeting memory.

The realization that we are pilgrims on a journey toward a home with God can be quite disconcerting because we want to be somewhere, and to feel stable and safe. Instead, we are always moving on in some way. I have strong memories of canoe trips, some of them quite lengthy. I can recall "perfect" camp sites into which we "settled" and made home for a time. With a fire, welcome food and the shelter of a secure tent, we felt we belonged on that point, or bay, and became part of the landscape.

There was always the time, though, when we had to move on and break camp, as our journey had to continue and we had to set out anew. It was always with some regrets that we left the security of that perfect spot and dismantled the stuff of our security there. And yet we moved on, and later there was another place to settle until we finally came to the end of our journey.

The canoe trip is a good illustration of the Christian life; it is a life of journey entered into by travellers, or pilgrims. As resistant as we are to change and growth, that is nevertheless our calling. Until we arrive home with God, we are always breaking camp in order to move on. There is one true "home" for believers and the work of aging is to live more and more in anticipation of that arrival. Our task is not to await the end of things, but to seek the new beginning the journey always offers us.

> *Yes, we do have confidence, and we would rather be away from the body and at home with the Lord.*
> [2Cor.5.8; NRSV]

Y.

Yearning

ONE OF THE WRITERS of Isaiah, and hymn-writers over many decades, have spoken about their soul yearning to see God. I do not have that kind of yearning, at least not with that sense of inner desire. The fact that I have just said that, however, gives me pangs of guilt and fear. Why is wishing to be in God's presence not something closer to the surface of my longing? The readers of the Old Testament world knew that to see the face of God meant death to any human being, so I suppose I can imagine that they might have had a deep yearning to do just that. For new covenant believers such as myself, though, the Incarnation has prepared us for such an intimacy. I need to think and maybe challenge my hesitancy.

As a deer longs for flowing streams, so my soul longs for you, O God. [Ps. 42.1; NRSV]

Youthfulness

As AN OLD MAN, the artist Picasso noted that "it takes a very long time to become young." His words echo the common sentiment that youth is usually wasted on the young and that it is only in the fullness of life that meaning is accessible to us. What youth possesses in terms of energy and nerve, it unfortunately often lacks in terms of wisdom and experience. The paradox is that while the young spend time making mistakes and building an inventory of things learned, the more elderly often fail to put to work their wisdom because they're moaning about their circumstances, aches and pains.

It's been said that the last third of life is a time to explore what life is about and it should be done with the verve and excitement of the young. What some have called the Third Act is a time when we're free to respond out of our wisdom, wholeness and our authentic selves. We're able to reflect from the base of maturity that comes with this Act. We are freed to be ourselves and contribute our understanding. It is not a time to complain about aging; rather it's a time to claim our youthfulness.

> *Bless the Lord, O my soul . . . who satisfies you with good as long as you live, so that your youth is renewed like the eagle's. [Ps.103. 1-5; NRSV]*

Z.

Zebras

OVER THE LAST DECADE of my teaching years at seminary, I had the good fortune to lead practicum trips to East Africa, primarily Kenya. This involved going for the month of August every other year, some six or so times. In that month, students were placed in various, supervised ministry settings in order to experience life and work in the East African Church. These were often challenging living conditions for our students, but they were also generally rich learning experiences as well. In the last few days, as the students re-gathered to recover, debrief and rest, we also included a short trip to Maasai Mara, at the Kenyan end of the vast Serengeti Plane.

This was an awesome experience in which one actually experienced one's childhood books of the animals of the world in all their glory. I sometimes felt I was experiencing the Garden of Eden itself. In many ways, it was the herds of zebras interwoven with wildebeest that struck me the most. What whimsical creator conceived the zebra? And don't answer me with natural selection; not even that can explain the striped bodies of the zebra. The more I looked at them the more amazed I was at their diversity of design and decoration.

The more outrageous our God's design the more I realize that, being in the image of God, we're nevertheless pale imitations of what God really is like. We can never reach into the future and imagine what God will make of us there, either. Our minds and creative capacity are just too limited. Maybe we shouldn't worry about it so much. Whatever God makes of us in eternity will be just fine!

Let the earth bring forth living creatures of every kind: cattle and creeping things and wild animals of the earth of every kind. [Gen. 1.24; NRSV]

ENDNOTES

[1] Bette Davis.

[2] This famous Macdonalds slogan was actually coined in 1971!

[3] Henri J. M. Nouwen, *Life of the Beloved: Spiritual Living in a Secular World.*

[4] Ibid.

[5] *Waking Ned Divine* (1998).

[6] Joseph Bayley, *Heaven.*

[7] Samuel Beckett, *Waiting for Godot.*

[8] Many are listed as users of this saying. Perhaps one of the earliest was Francis Bacon.

[9] *The Cloud of Unknowing* was written in the latter half of the 14th Century, in Middle English.

[10] That I still remember my father's exact response to my 99% on a Greek mythology test suggests the power of his disapproval.

[11] Annie Dillard, *Pilgrim at Tinker Creek*, 1974.

[12] Gratitude in an oft repeated theme in Nouwen's work; *Radical Gratitude* (2002) is an important book by Mary Jo Leddy on the same quality.

[13] Xanadu is the subject of *Kublai Khan*, Samuel Taylor Coleridge, 1797.

[14] This a well-known saying of the painter Pablo Picasso (1881-1973).